Introduction to Research Tools

Introduction to Research Tools

STUDY & LEARNING

Published by
Heron Books, Inc.
20950 SW Rock Creek Road
Sheridan, OR 97378

heronbooks.com

Special thanks to all the teachers and students who
provided feedback instrumental to this edition.

Third Edition © 1987, 2023 Heron Books.
All Rights Reserved

ISBN: 978-0-89-739337-9

Any unauthorized copying, translation, duplication or distribution, in whole
or in part, by any means, including electronic copying, storage or transmission,
is a violation of applicable laws.

The Heron Books name and the heron bird symbol are registered trademarks
of Delphi Schools, Inc.

Printed in the USA

20 May 2023

At Heron Books, we think learning should be engaging and fun. It should be hands-on and allow students to move at their own pace.

To facilitate this we have created a learning guide that will help any student progress through this book, chapter by chapter, with confidence and interest.

Get learning guides at
heronbooks.com/learningguides.

For teacher resources,
such as a final exam, email
teacherresources@heronbooks.com.

We would love to hear from you!
Email us at *feedback@heronbooks.com*.

CONTENTS

CHAPTER 1

Why Research? 3
    What Do You Want to Know? 3
    Activity: Create Research Questions. 5

CHAPTER 2

Types of Research Data 9
    Activity: Create Questions for Second-Hand Research 11
    Activity: Observe Differences in Third-Hand Data 12

CHAPTER 3

Using Accurate Research Data 15
    First-Hand Data Accuracy. 15
    Second- and Third-Hand Data Accuracy 16

CHAPTER 4

How to Research 19
    Writing Research Reports 20

CHAPTER 5

Using the Internet 23
Internet Service 23
Browsing the Internet 24
Searching the Internet 25
Searching With Google 27
Activity: Searching the Internet 28

CHAPTER 6

Ensuring You Have True Data from the Internet 31
Ways To Verify Internet Data 32
Activity: Verifying Internet Information 34

CHAPTER 1
Why Research?

CHAPTER 1

Why Research?

When you look for information, that is **research**. When you ask questions and search for answers by observing and discovering things, you are researching. When you do an experiment, that is research too. Research is not just looking up information that others have found. It is also a careful study of some subject or part of life to discover new facts or make new conclusions about it.

Because things in the world can change so fast, it is useful to be able to do quick and accurate studies of subjects. This is true of most subjects from literature to science.

If you can accurately observe and really understand something you are researching, you have a better chance of making correct decisions about it. That enables you to judge how to change within this rapidly changing world.

In many subjects, there are not always exact answers to all questions, and you cannot always find the answers in books. Being able to research effectively will allow you to get the answers you are looking for.

WHAT DO YOU WANT TO KNOW?

All research starts with a question—yours or someone else's. A good research question asks for the exact information that will guide you to complete the research fully.

WHY RESEARCH?

Once you have the question, it's time to carefully investigate or observe facts or truths about your subject. Research is observing, examining and questioning what you find. Then you must evaluate what you find by figuring out how reliable the sources of information are, and also how valuable and useful the data is.

The purpose of research is always to make new discoveries or find new answers.

What you discover could simply be new data to you, such as when you research a question about history. Or it could be new data to humankind, such as when doctors are researching a disease to learn how to cure it.

An effective researcher will create the exact question they want answered to achieve the purpose of the research. This may naturally lead to other questions.

For example, when doctors are researching how to cure a disease, they may start with the question, "What germ causes this disease, and how can people be protected from it?" Once that is discovered, they may want to know, "Do medicines exist that kill that germ without harming the body?" Once they have an answer to that question, more questions will follow until they discover how to cure the disease.

Start each research project with a question that will get the data you need.

ACTIVITY
Create Research Questions

For this activity, you will need

- notebook and pen or pencil

Information

This activity will give you a chance to practice creating questions that will effectively guide some research. Here is an example:

I'm observing a basketball game and wonder if I could play that sport. I want to research this and think of these questions:

Why is the basketball that big?

What is the net made of?

Neither of those questions would guide my research about what is needed to play basketball.

I need to ask precise questions in line with the purpose of my research. Here are some questions that would do that:

What main skills do basketball players need?

I'm tall for my age so I want to research: Do tall players need different skills than shorter players?

Now it's your turn to create some effective research questions.

WHY RESEARCH?

Steps

1. With your notebook and pen, look around and find an area that looks interesting to you. It can be indoors or outdoors. Explore anything you are curious about.

2. While you're exploring, notice some things you've never noticed before. Think of what you want to know about one of those things. Write down three or four questions you have about that thing.

3. Review your questions and decide which one asks precisely for the data you want to know.

4. If none of your questions get the exact data you want to know, create some new questions until you have one that asks for the exact information you want to find out.

5. Find another area that looks interesting to you. Do the same thing. Explore it. Notice some things you've never noticed before, and think of three or four questions you have about one of these things. Write down your questions about that thing.

6. Review your questions and decide which one asks precisely for the data you want to know.

7. If none of your questions get the exact data you want to know, create some new questions until you have one that asks for the exact information you need to find out.

8. When you're all done, tell someone what all research starts with, and explain why. Then describe the questions you created for this activity and say which ones you thought were the best, and what you learned.

CHAPTER 2
Types of Research Data

CHAPTER 2

Types of Research Data

There are three main categories of data to use in research:

- first-hand data,
- second-hand data,
- third-hand data.

When you answer a research question by observing the subject yourself, you are using first-hand data. **First-hand data** means it has been learned by direct observation[1] of the subject. You may have done this at some time by doing a science experiment and learning something new from the results.

When you use data from someone who personally observed or discovered it, you are researching with **second-hand data**. It is necessary to note the source (the person or reference you are getting the data from) in writing a research report.

---

1 **direct observation** means that *you* look, *you* study, *you* figure out.

TYPES OF RESEARCH DATA

Third-hand data is further removed from the source of the information because the person or reference you are learning it from got it from someone else. The data may have come through a lot of people or books before you found it. Often this data comes from encyclopedias, books, the internet, or another person who learned it from someone else. It is third-hand data because you are learning about it from someone who did not observe it directly.

You're probably familiar with a research assignment where a question is given, and you look for answers in books or on the internet. This is using information that other people have found out. It is usually third-hand data.

When you use second-hand or third-hand data, you are taking someone else's word for what happened. This does not mean it is bad data--often it is excellent data. You just have to verify that the data is accurate, especially with data from the internet.

There is so much to know that sometimes you will want to use information from second- and third-hand sources when you are researching, especially if it isn't possible to find out for yourself.

If you observe accurately and report honestly, it's easy to be sure about the accuracy of first-hand data. It's faster to use valid second- or third-hand data. The trick is knowing how to find and evaluate the accuracy of that data.

TYPES OF RESEARCH DATA

ACTIVITY
Create Questions for Second-Hand Research

For this activity you will need

- a person to talk to who has lived in or visited another country
- your notebook and a pen or pencil

Steps

1. Think of several questions that will help you learn about the person's experiences in the other country, and write your questions down.

2. Review your questions and decide which one asks most precisely for the data you want to know about the country or the person's experiences there.

3. Talk to the person who has lived in or visited another country, and ask all of your questions. Take notes of what you learn.

4. Optional: If none of your questions get the exact data you want to know, create some new questions that ask for the exact information you need to find out. Write your questions down.

5. Optional: Go back to the same person and ask your new questions. Take notes of what you learn.

6. When you're all done, tell another person about the questions you created, which one you thought was the best, and what you learned.

TYPES OF RESEARCH DATA

ACTIVITY
Observe Differences in Third-Hand Data

For this activity, you will need

- computer with access to the internet
- notebook and pen or pencil

Steps

1. Go to sweetsearch.com and search for:

    average salary for a doctor

2. Several references will be listed. Look at three to five of them, and write down the different answers given along with the sources.

3. Again on sweetsearch.com, search for:

    length of Nile River

4. Look at three to five of the references given and write down the different answers given along with the sources.

5. Tell your instructor why you think there are different answers to the same question. For the two searches, explain which reference you found most useful.

CHAPTER 3
Using Accurate Research Data

CHAPTER 3

Using Accurate Research Data

Accurate data is specific, true, and free from errors and false information. Obviously, it is the only kind of data you want to use in your research.

FIRST-HAND DATA ACCURACY

When you research by direct observation, you have to make good observations and careful measurements to be accurate in your results. There are two sides to this:

1. Carefully observing and measuring the data to ensure it is accurate.

2. Ensuring no false or omitted data enters into your results.

The first point is clear, but the second might be a bit surprising. People sometimes violate this because of laziness or because they don't like the data they find.

For example, suppose a person decided to prove that lemon trees grow faster than orange trees, and started an experiment to research this. Suppose the orange trees grew faster, in fact. If the researcher observes accurately, they will change their idea that lemon trees grow faster, use the data discovered,

USING ACCURATE RESEARCH DATA

and report it accurately. If they don't like the outcome and decide to hide the true data, or report the opposite results to support their original opinion, they would add false information and destroy the accuracy of their research.

Accuracy in first-hand data includes good observation without adding any opinions or other ideas to change or falsify the facts.

SECOND- AND THIRD-HAND DATA ACCURACY

When you use someone else's data, it is important to know how accurate it is. Sometimes it is data you can test for workability, as you would do in science experiment. Other times, you can compare the data to another source of data that you trust.

It is harder to be sure the data is correct when you don't already know a lot about the area, but you can rely on certain references. For instance, encyclopedias are verified sources of information while tabloid[2] newspapers generally are not. Always evaluate how trustworthy the source of data is.

When you use materials written by others, make sure the data seems true and makes sense to you. With practice you'll learn to recognize true data and ignore false information.

This is the researcher's responsibility—when you use data or give the data you found to others, be as accurate as you can. When you aren't sure how true some second-hand or third-hand data is, find another source of information that you can trust.

Accuracy comes into both your research and your report about it.

The best rule for research is:

observe carefully and report honestly.

---

2   **tabloid**: a newspaper printed on small sheets, usually half the ordinary size. Tabloids usually contain big headlines, many pictures, and wild, unbelievable stories.

CHAPTER 4
How to Research

CHAPTER 4

How to Research

First, form your research question or name the problem you want to solve. If you are assigned a research question to explore, ensure you understand the question, and what information you're looking for.

Start researching the subject by studying any first- and second-hand data that is available. Then find and use applicable third-hand data. Choose data that you can read and understand well. If the information is too hard to read, find another source that is easier to read.

Keep notes. Some people write in notebooks, and others keep notes on their computer. However you decide to keep notes of your research data, do it so you know the source of each piece of information you're using and can find it again when needed.

Continue to search and find answers. As you collect data, form more detailed questions to find all the exact data you need. Write down your questions in your notes.

Don't believe everything you read, especially on the internet. Before accepting data found, determine that the information you want to use is true data.

Check the information you find against other sources to verify that it is accurate.

HOW TO RESEARCH

WRITING RESEARCH REPORTS

When writing a research report, put it in your own words. Report on the question or questions you started with, and the information you found in a logical sequence. Include your own exploration of the subject, and any conclusions you made or solutions you came up with.

If you directly use or quote another's research, note the verified source of the quote in your report by saying where you found it. Usually, you put this information in parentheses right after the quote or data. This is called **citing** the source. If you're using someone else's original idea, even if it's not an exact quote, cite the source of that information too.

You don't have to cite a specific source if you are using information or ideas that are common knowledge. For example, it is common knowledge that Christopher Columbus sailed to the New World in 1492, so it is fine to use that fact in a report without citing the reference where you found that data.

If some data you find in your research is not common knowledge, then you must cite the source of the data like this:

> In 1504, Columbus had knowledge of an upcoming solar eclipse and used it to terrify the natives in the New World so they would obey him. (www.history.com/news/10-things-you-may-not-know-about-christopher-columbus)

Failing to cite someone else's original idea or information in a report is a form of stealing another person's work. It is dishonest research.

Honesty in reporting on research means you give credit to others for their original ideas by citing where you found their data. Then you include your own thoughts, conclusions, and solutions based on your research.

CHAPTER 5

Using the Internet

CHAPTER 5

Using the Internet

A **computer network** is a system of computers that are linked together through cables, satellites, and other ways.

The **internet** is an enormous computer network that links together millions of computers around the world so that they can communicate to each other.

A computer is not automatically connected to the internet, but when it is on the internet, it is linked to all the other computers on the internet and can share information with them.

The **world wide web** (abbreviated www, or called web for short) is a connected system of written pages that anyone can access through the internet. It uses the internet but is not the same as the internet. The internet computers carry the pages on the world wide web. These pages are called websites. A **website** is a collection of pages on the world wide web that you access under one name.

Over a billion pages of information and computer programs are stored in computers that are on the internet.

INTERNET SERVICE

To get on the internet, you need the necessary connections using telephone lines or wireless links. The companies that provide this are called **Internet**

USING THE INTERNET

Service Providers or *ISP*s. An **ISP** is a business that provides access to the internet, usually for a monthly charge. Comcast and Verizon are examples, but there are many others. If your computer is set up to access the internet, then you already have an ISP. Large ISPs also may provide extra internet services to their subscribers, including news, weather, and entertainment.

BROWSING THE INTERNET

To **browse** means to look through a book, website, or something similar without reading everything. To locate and sort through the many webpages on the internet, you use a computer program called a **browser**. This allows you to browse the pages of the world wide web once the computer is connected to the internet. At this writing, Google Chrome, Apple Safari, and Microsoft Edge are the most common browsers.

When you start the browser on your computer, it connects your computer to the Internet.

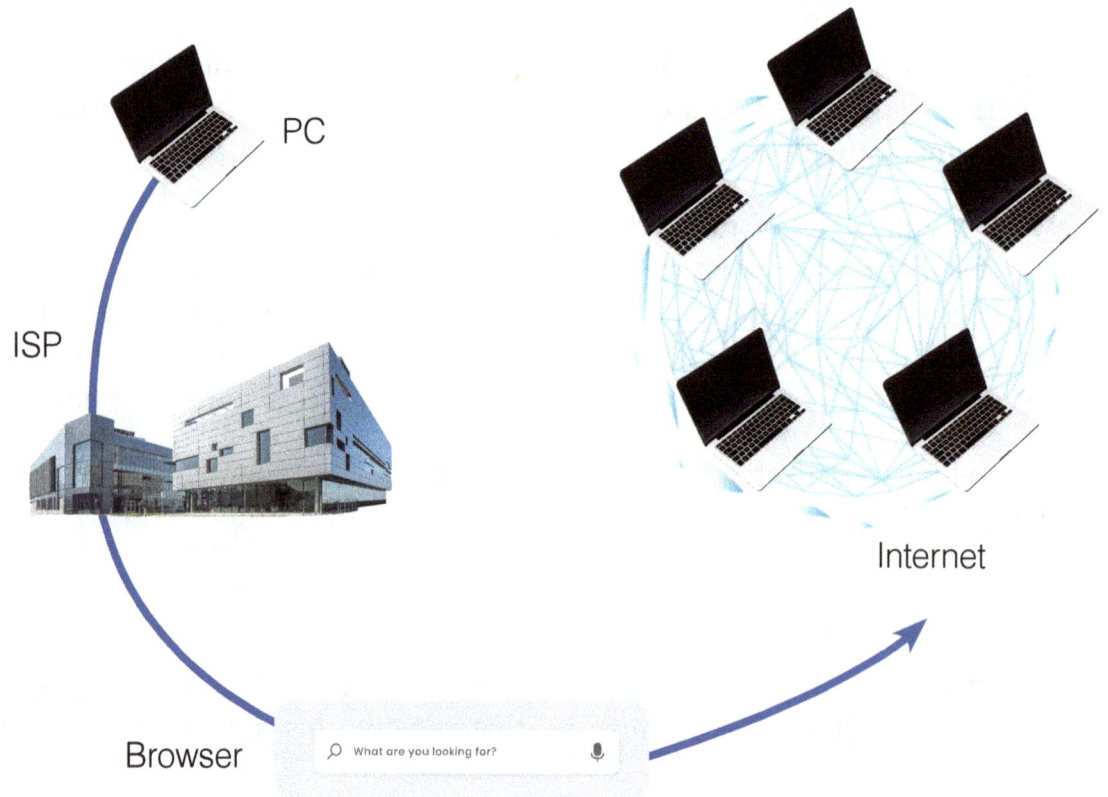

24

USING THE INTERNET

SEARCHING THE INTERNET

To search the internet for specific information you need for your research projects, you will use a search engine. A **search engine** is a program that allows you to quickly search for specific information in the web pages. In America, Google is the most-used search engine, but Microsoft Bing, Yahoo, DuckDuckGo (for privacy protection), and Ask.com are some other search engines. In other parts of the world, Baidu (Chinese) and Yandex (Russian) are commonly used.

There are also search engines for kids that are easy to use. As of this writing, some of the better ones are Sweet Search, and Ask Jeeves for Kids.

A search engine looks for key words[3] in the web pages and then gives you a list of websites and web pages that contain the key words.

For instance, suppose you wanted to find out about kangaroos. When you type the word *kangaroo* in the search engine bar, you will get a list of all the websites that contain the word kangaroo. The search engine also will give you a link to go directly to any website or web page on the list so that you can study it.

You can find a lot of information fast by researching subjects on the internet, but it takes some practice. If you're researching a very specific subject, the search engine may find just a few pages for you to look at. However, for a broad subject like *cowboys,* there will be too many web pages to read, and they will be on more than one subject. (If you type in the word *cowboys,* you might get a list of web pages that has information about the Dallas Cowboys football team, real cowboys today, movies about cowboys, and more.)

---

[3] A **key word** is a basic or important word in a subject. It serves as a guide to the subject of the web page.

USING THE INTERNET

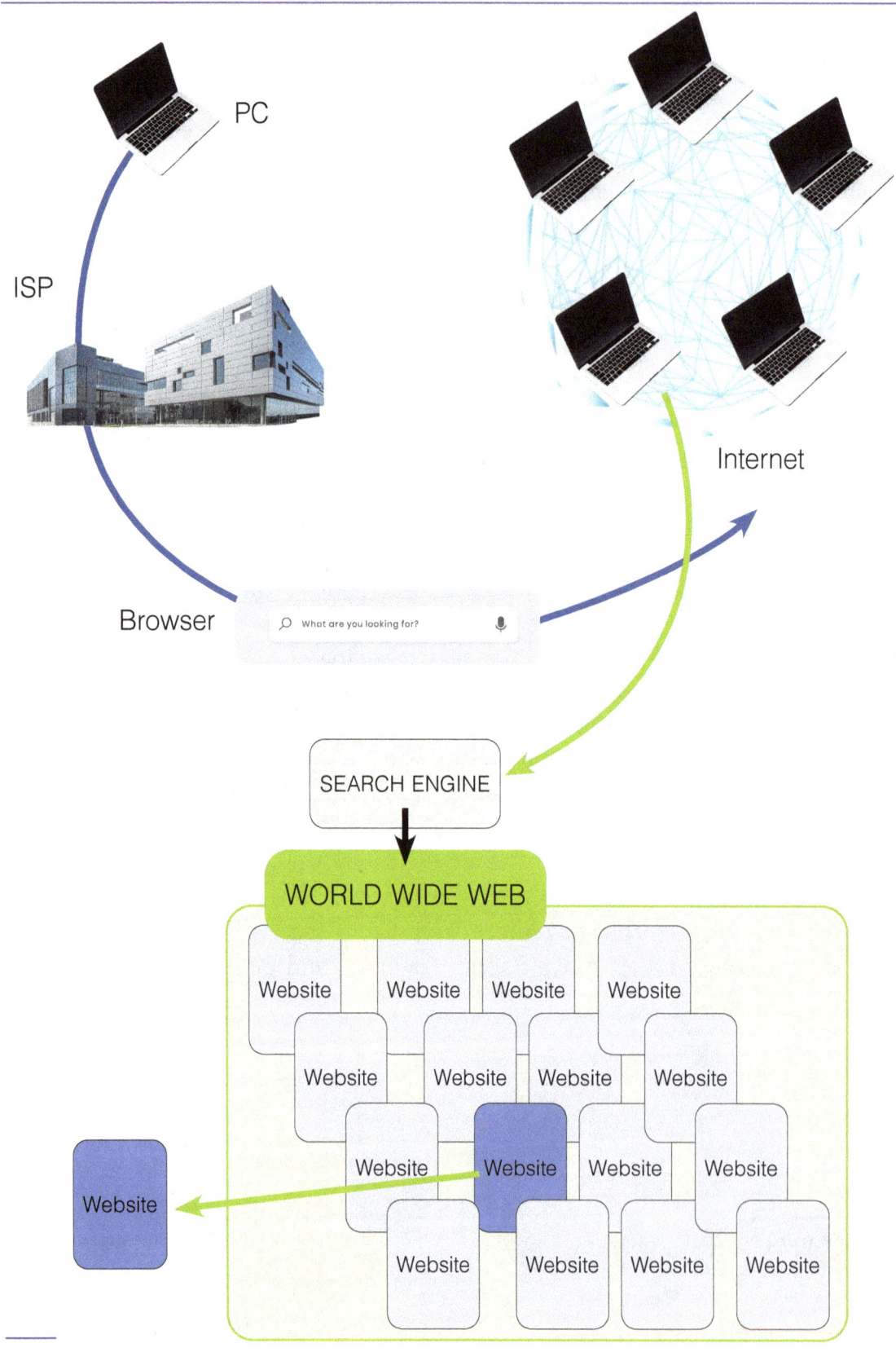

There are ways to limit your search so that you don't get every web page on a subject when you're looking for specific ones that have the information you want. You do this by figuring out the exact key words to type into your search engine.

If you want to learn more about how to do internet searches, view a **tutorial**, video instructions that teach you how to do it. There are several good ones on YouTube.

SEARCHING WITH GOOGLE

Because Google's search engine is the most commonly used, here are some tips on finding what you want using Google.

Start the search by typing in important, key words. Don't worry about punctuation.

If the initial results don't give you the data you want, try adding to or changing the key words.

Use the search results to give you clues on key words or questions to ask to narrow the search and find the exact data you want.

If you want to search for words in an exact order, type them into the search bar in quotation marks.

There is so much information available on the internet that you have plenty of data at your fingertips. The challenge is finding applicable, true data that is easy to read out of all the information given in your search.

USING THE INTERNET

ACTIVITY
Searching the Internet

For this activity you will need

- computer with access to the internet

Steps

1. Think of a topic you are interested in knowing more about.

2. Type key words into the Goggle search bar.

3. Click on the link to one of the references that appears to have the information you want.

4. Read the first paragraph or two and determine if this reference is too hard to read or doesn't have the data you are looking for.

5. If it's not useful, click the back arrow to return to the list of references and choose another reference.

6. Keep searching until you find a readable, useful reference for your research.

7. Tell someone what you did to find a useful reference.

CHAPTER 6

Ensuring You Have True Data from the Internet

CHAPTER 6

Ensuring You Have True Data from the Internet

You can find a lot of very good data on the internet, but there is also false or illogical information that can mislead a researcher. With a reference like an encyclopedia, a whole team of people ensure the information is verified and free from errors.

There is no one making sure all the data put on the internet is correct, however.

People can put almost anything on the internet they want. Sometimes incorrect data is written on web pages because the person writing it thought it was correct, but they were mistaken. And sometimes people deliberately put false information on the internet. There may be several reasons for doing this, such as wanting people to believe the same things they believe, wanting to mislead people, misunderstanding the subject, and so on.

Because of this, researchers using information from the internet must always verify that data to ensure it is true and complete.

ENSURING YOU HAVE TRUE DATA FROM THE INTERNET

WAYS TO VERIFY INTERNET DATA

When you have Google search for information regarding your research question or subject, it will list some websites. Now it's your responsibility to verify the data on these websites. Here are some steps that can help with this:

1. Choose one of the websites listed from your search. Briefly read over the information given.

2. Make sure the information is easy enough to read. If it's too hard to read, go to another website.

3. Make sure the information is up-to-date. Often articles on websites have dates, which can help with this. If you need to, go to another website.

4. Once you find a reference that is up-to-date and easy to read, make sure you understand all the words in it or clear up any you don't understand.

5. Decide if this information answers all or part of your research question. If it doesn't answer any part of your question, go to another website and start over.

6. If all looks good so far, keep that website open. Click on one of the other websites listed by your search engine, and do steps 1-5 with it. If all looks correct, check the information from the first website against the second website to see if the data matches. If it does, that most likely verifies that the data is accurate.

7. If you are still not sure about the information, open a third website from the list and check the data against it.

8. Make notes of any verified information you want to use in your research, including the websites and authors that are the source of the data.

As you gain experience and skill searching the internet, you will recognize that some websites are never to be relied upon for accurate data and you can avoid them. On the other hand, you will learn that there are websites that reliably contain true data.

If you use a search engine for kids like Sweet Search, there is a team of people verifying any data they list in the search results. This makes your job easier, but you still have to make sure the data is logical and answers your research question.

Sometimes you can verify internet data with someone who personally knows the subject. For example, you may be researching the best design for an airplane and you know someone who works in that business. Or you are researching a historical event that your grandfather was part of. Then you can discuss the information you found to verify it.

So, verifying internet information may not be necessary with a specialized search engine for kids, like Sweet Search. But when searching the internet broadly with Google or another search engine, always verify the information you find.

Research really is a game of digging out data, learning, and verifying new facts. Think of all the new things you'll be able to explore and discover!

ENSURING YOU HAVE TRUE DATA FROM THE INTERNET

ACTIVITY
Verifying Internet Information

For this activity, you will need

- computer with access to the internet

Steps

1. Decide on something you want to research.

2. Type keywords in the Google search bar.

3. Choose a website and briefly read over the information given.

4. Make sure the information is easy enough to read. If it's too hard to read, go to another website.

5. Make sure the information is up-to-date. Often articles on websites have dates, which can help with this. If you need to, go to another website.

6. Once you find a reference that is up-to-date and easy to read, make sure you understand all the words in it or clear up any you need to.

7. Decide if this information answers all or part of your research question. If it doesn't answer any part of your question, go to another website and start over.

8. If all looks good so far, keep that website open. Click on one of the other websites listed by your search engine, and do steps 1-7 with it. If all looks correct, check the information from the first website against the second website to see if the data matches. If it does, that most likely verifies that the data is accurate.

9. If you are still not sure about the information, open a third website from the list and check the data against it.

10. Make notes of any verified information you want to use in your research, including the websites and authors that are the source of the data.

www.ingramcontent.com/pod-product-compliance
Lightning Source LLC
Chambersburg PA
CBHW081354040426
42450CB00016B/3441